the NUTCRACKER *for* EASY PIANO

Arranged by David Pearl
Additional arranging by John Nicholas

Cherry Lane Music Company
Director of Publications/Project Editor: Mark Phillips

ISBN 978-1-60378-318-7

Visit our website at www.cherrylane.com

Overture

By Pyotr Il'yich Tchaikovsky

D.C. al Coda

Coda

cresc.

March

By Pyotr Il'yich Tchaikovsky

5

The Land of Sweets (Confiturembourg)

By Pyotr Il'yich Tchaikovsky

D.C. (with repeat) al Coda

Coda

Spanish Dance ("Chocolate")

By Pyotr Il'yich Tchaikovsky

Arabian Dance ("Coffee")

By Pyotr Il'yich Tchaikovsky

Moderately

14

Chinese Dance ("Tea")

By Pyotr Il'yich Tchaikovsky

Russian Dance ("Trepak")

By Pyotr Il'yich Tchaikovsky

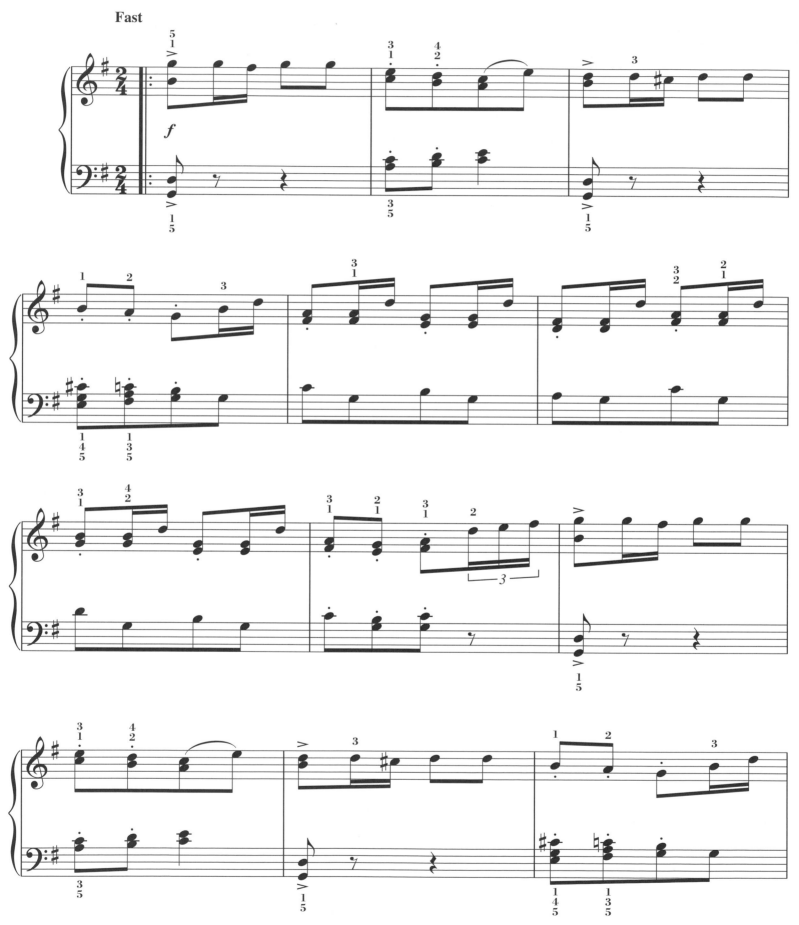

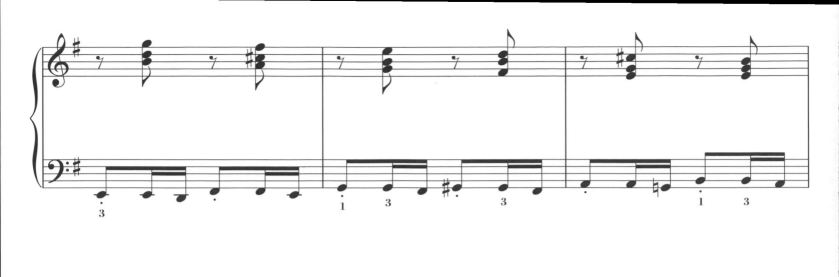

D.C. al Coda

Dance of the Reed-Flutes

By Pyotr Il'yich Tchaikovsky

Waltz of the Flowers

By Pyotr Il'yich Tchaikovsky

Moderately slow, in 1

Dance of the Sugar Plum Fairy

By Pyotr Il'yich Tchaikovsky

To Coda

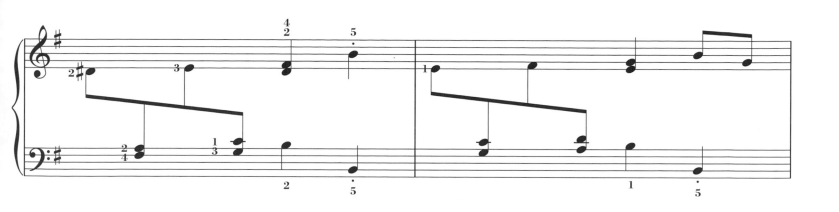

D.C. al Coda

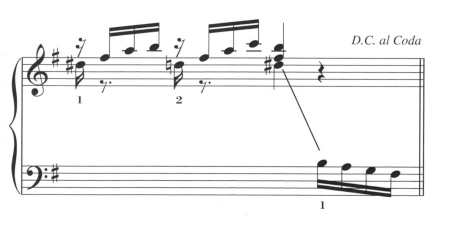

Coda

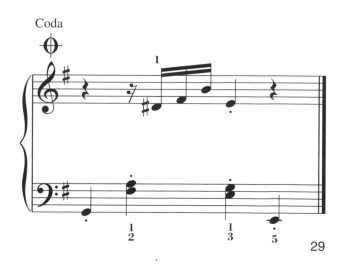

Pas de Deux

By Pyotr Il'yich Tchaikovsky

Final Waltz

By Pyotr Il'yich Tchaikovsky

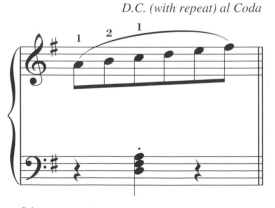

D.C. (with repeat) al Coda

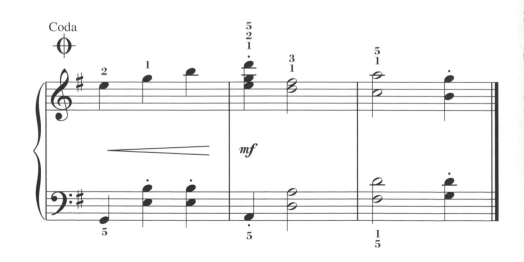

Coda

mf

34

CHRISTMAS COLLECTIONS
FROM HAL LEONARD
ALL BOOKS ARRANGED FOR PIANO, VOICE & GUITAR

THE BEST CHRISTMAS SONGS EVER

69 all-time favorites: Auld Lang Syne • Coventry Carol • Frosty the Snow Man • Happy Holiday • It Came Upon the Midnight Clear • O Holy Night • Rudolph the Red-Nosed Reindeer • Silver Bells • What Child Is This? • and many more.

00359130 ....$29.99

THE BIG BOOK OF CHRISTMAS SONGS

Over 120 all-time favorites and hard-to-find classics: As Each Happy Christmas • The Boar's Head Carol • Carol of the Bells • Deck the Halls • The Friendly Beasts • God Rest Ye Merry Gentlemen • Joy to the World • Masters in This Hall • O Holy Night • Story of the Shepherd • and more.

00311520 ....$22.99

CHRISTMAS SONGS – BUDGET BOOKS

100 holiday favorites: All I Want for Christmas Is You • Christmas Time Is Here • Feliz Navidad • Grandma Got Run Over by a Reindeer • I'll Be Home for Christmas • Last Christmas • O Holy Night • Please Come Home for Christmas • Rockin' Around the Christmas Tree • We Need a Little Christmas • What Child Is This? • and more.

00310887 ....$15.99

CHRISTMAS MOVIE SONGS

34 holiday hits from the big screen: All I Want for Christmas Is You • Believe • Christmas Vacation • Do You Want to Build a Snowman? • Frosty the Snow Man • Have Yourself a Merry Little Christmas • It's Beginning to Look like Christmas • Mele Kalikimaka • Rudolph the Red-Nosed Reindeer • Silver Bells • White Christmas • You're a Mean One, Mr. Grinch • and more.

00146961 ....$19.99

CHRISTMAS PIANO SONGS FOR DUMMIES®

56 favorites: Auld Lang Syne • Away in a Manger • Blue Christmas • The Christmas Song • Deck the Hall • I'll Be Home for Christmas • Jingle Bells • Joy to the World • My Favorite Things • Silent Night • more!

00311387 ....$19.95

CHRISTMAS POP STANDARDS

22 contemporary holiday hits, including: All I Want for Christmas Is You • Christmas Time Is Here • Little Saint Nick • Mary, Did You Know? • Merry Christmas, Darling • Santa Baby • Underneath the Tree • Where Are You Christmas? • and more.

00348998 ....$14.99

CHRISTMAS SING-ALONG

40 seasonal favorites: Away in a Manger • Christmas Time Is Here • Feliz Navidad • Happy Holiday • Jingle Bells • Mary, Did You Know? • O Come, All Ye Faithful • Rudolph the Red-Nosed Reindeer • Silent Night • White Christmas • and more. Includes online sing-along backing tracks.

00278176 Book/Online Audio $24.99

100 CHRISTMAS CAROLS

Includes: Away in a Manger • Bring a Torch, Jeannette, Isabella • Coventry Carol • Deck the Hall • The First Noel • Go, Tell It on the Mountain • I Heard the Bells on Christmas Day • Joy to the World • O Come, All Ye Faithful (Adeste Fideles) • Silent Night • Sing We Now of Christmas • and more.

00310897 ....$19.99

100 MOST BEAUTIFUL CHRISTMAS SONGS

Includes: Angels We Have Heard on High • Baby, It's Cold Outside • Christmas Time Is Here • Do You Hear What I Hear • Grown-Up Christmas List • Happy Xmas (War Is Over) • I'll Be Home for Christmas • The Little Drummer Boy • Mary, Did You Know? • O Holy Night • White Christmas • Winter Wonderland • and more.

00237285 ....$27.99

POPULAR CHRISTMAS SHEET MUSIC: 1980-2017

40 recent seasonal favorites: All I Want for Christmas Is You • Because It's Christmas (For All the Children) • Breath of Heaven (Mary's Song) • Christmas Lights • The Christmas Shoes • The Gift • Grown-Up Christmas List • Last Christmas • Santa Tell Me • Snowman • Where Are You Christmas? • Wrapped in Red • and more.

00278089 ....$22.99

A SENTIMENTAL CHRISTMAS BOOK

27 beloved Christmas favorites, including: The Christmas Shoes • The Christmas Song (Chestnuts Roasting on an Open Fire) • Christmas Time Is Here • Grown-Up Christmas List • Have Yourself a Merry Little Christmas • I'll Be Home for Christmas • Somewhere in My Memory • Where Are You Christmas? • and more.

00236830 ....$14.99

ULTIMATE CHRISTMAS

100 seasonal favorites: Auld Lang Syne • Bring a Torch, Jeannette, Isabella • Carol of the Bells • The Chipmunk Song • Christmas Time Is Here • The First Noel • Frosty the Snow Man • Gesù Bambino • Happy Holiday • Happy Xmas (War Is Over) • Jingle-Bell Rock • Pretty Paper • Silver Bells • Suzy Snowflake • and more.

00361399 ....$24.99

A VERY MERRY CHRISTMAS

39 familiar favorites: Blue Christmas • Feliz Navidad • Happy Xmas (War Is Over) • I'll Be Home for Christmas • Jingle-Bell Rock • Please Come Home for Christmas • Rockin' Around the Christmas Tree • Santa, Bring My Baby Back (To Me) • Sleigh Ride • White Christmas • and more.

00310536 ....$14.99

HAL•LEONARD®

Complete contents listings available online at www.halleonard.com

PRICES, CONTENTS, AND AVAILABILITY SUBJECT
TO CHANGE WITHOUT NOTICE.

YOUR FAVORITE CLASSICAL MUSIC FOR EASY PIANO

21 Great Classics
The Phillip Keveren Series
Features 21 beloved classical masterworks by famous composers arranged for easy piano by Phillip Keveren. Includes: Air on the G String • Can Can • Canon in D Major • Eine Kleine Nachtmusik • La donna è mobile • and more.
00310717 .... $12.99

Easy Classics
18 classical masterworks from composers like Bach, Beethoven, Bizet, Brahms, Schubert, Verdi and others. Selections include: Ave Maria • Canon in D Major • Für Elise • Liebestraum • Habanera • Ode to Joy • Sicilienne • and more.
00240217 .... $8.99

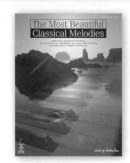

The Most Beautiful Classical Melodies
46 classical favorites: Air on the G String (Bach) • Canon in D (Pachelbel) • Jesu, Joy of Man's Desiring (Bach) • Panis Angelicus (O Lord Most Holy) (Franck) • Pomp and Circumstance (Elgar) • and more.
02500095 .... $12.99

50 Easy Classical Themes
Easy arrangements of 50 classical tunes from 30 composers: Bach, Beethoven, Chopin, Debussy, Handel, Haydn, Liszt, Mozart, Puccini, Rossini, Schubert, Strauss, Tchaikovsky, Vivaldi and more.
00311215 .... $14.99

First 50 Baroque Pieces You Should Play on Piano
Includes: Air (Air on the G String) (J.S. Bach) • Jesu, Joy of Man's Desiring (J.S. Bach) • Lullaby in F Major (Kirnberger) • March in D Major (J.S. Bach) • Minuet in G Major (J.S. Bach) • more.
00291453 .... $15.99

My First Classical Song Book
34 famous classical melodies, each illustrated with color photography of great paintings. Contents: Arioso • Toccata & Fugue in D min • Fur Elise • Hungarian Dance No. 5 • Lullaby • Meditation • and more.
00312532 .... $17.99

50 Most Popular Classical Melodies
Easy arrangements of beloved pieces including: Ave Maria • By the Beautiful Blue Danube • Canon in D • Clair De Lune • Dance of the Sugar Plum Fairy • Für Elise • Hallelujah Chorus • Moonlight Sonata • and dozens of others.
02501401 .... $16.99

First 50 Classical Pieces You Should Play on the Piano
A great collection of must-know classics: Ave Maria (Schubert) • In the Hall of the Mountain King (Grieg) • Jesu, Joy of Man's Desiring (Bach) • Moonlight Sonata (Beethoven) • and more.
00131436 .... $15.99

The Piano Bench of Easy Classical Music
400 pages of great music literature, specially selected for the developing pianist. Includes: Air (Handel) • Habañera (Bizet) • Jesu, Joy of Man's Desiring (JS Bach) • Liebestraume (Liszt) • more.
14025483 .... $29.99

Classical Themes for Kids
25 timeless classical selections: The Flight of the Bumble Bee • Hornpipe • Liebestraum No. 3 • Pomp and Circumstance • Rhapsody in Blue • Toreador Song • William Tell Overture • more.
00346750 .... $10.99

Hooked on Easy Piano Classics
35 classics: Canon in D (Pachelbel) • The Entertainer (Joplin) • March Militaire (Schubert) • Moonlight Sonata (Beethoven) • Romeo and Juliet (Tchaikovsky) • Toreador Song (Bizet) • and more.
00004029 .... $14.99

Simple Classical Piano Pieces
Play 50 favorites by Bach, Beethoven, Mozart, and others that are perfect for beginners. Inclues: Aria • Dance In G Major • Little Rondo • Minuet • Rigaudon • Sonatina • Waltz, Op. 101, No. 1 • and more.
00288045 .... $9.99

Contemporary Piano Masters
This exceptional collection includes: Dawn from *Pride & Prejudice* (Dario Marianelli) • Fly (Ludovico Einaudi) • Game of Thrones Theme (Ramin Djawadi) • The Shape of Water Theme (Alexandre Desplat) • and more.
00290990 .... $19.99

The Library of Easy Piano Classics
A treasury of pieces that have captured the imagination of music lovers: Clair de Lune • Country Gardens • Melody in F • Pachelbel's Canon • Albeniz's Tango • and much more. Spiral bound.
14019031 .... $27.99

HAL•LEONARD®
www.halleonard.com